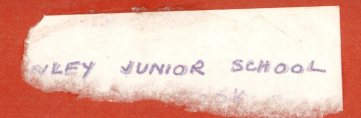

QUESTBOOKS

How life goes on

The butterfly
The frog
The duck

Where do things come from ?

Glass
Oil
Gold
Cotton

Tales from history

The flying balloon
The egg of Christopher Columbus
Diogenes and his lantern
The first train

Other titles are in preparation.

The first train

ISBN: 0 550 31903 4

Printed in Great Britain

English edition © W & R Chambers Ltd. Edinburgh, 1975
by arrangement with International Copyright Institute (ICI)

Tales from history

The first train

by Cyriel Verleyen
illustrated by Henry Branton

Chambers

It was the day before Christmas in England. The year was 1801. Samuel Smith was fast asleep, when suddenly a thumping, hissing sound woke him up. The sound grew louder.

People outside were shouting, 'Here it comes. Run for your lives!' The noise was terrible.

Samuel jumped up in bed. Black smoke rushed past his window. The lamp rattled on the table. The window rattled in its frame. Samuel even rattled in his bed.

'It must be the end of the world,' cried Samuel. He dressed himself quickly and ran outside.

A strange-looking waggon was passing by. It moved without horses, and smoke poured out of it.

However the driver looked happy. 'Fear not good people,' he said. 'It's perfectly safe.'

Then he pulled back the brake lever. It snapped in two. The waggon turned and crashed into a shop.

Samuel took out a pencil and paper. 'I am a newspaper reporter. Who are you sir, and *what* is that contraption?'

'I am the inventor Richard Trevithick. This is my horseless steam waggon.'

'Whark! Choof!' roared the waggon. And it began to move again.

'My waggon doesn't need horses. It's going to make me famous,' said Trevithick. Soon he was out of sight.

'Just look at my shop!' raged the shopkeeper. 'That man is raving mad. Nothing will ever replace horses.'

But Samuel was not so sure.

One day Samuel heard that Trevithick was in London to try out another steam waggon.

'I wonder what he's up to now?' thought Samuel. 'I'll go along and see.'

A large crowd was there when Samuel arrived. They were looking at a big steam waggon, which rested on wooden rails.

'My machine will ride on this wooden track,' said Trevithick. 'It will go faster than the wind.' Then he pushed a handle, and the wheels began to turn. All the people started cheering.

Suddenly the heavy waggon broke through the wooden track. It spluttered a little, then stopped dead. The cheers turned to laughter. Trevithick raised his hands in despair.

'Poor man,' thought Samuel. 'There's still a lot of work to be done, but some day I'm sure it will work.'

Years passed and Samuel heard
no more about steam waggons.

Then one day, while he was in the
town of Killingworth writing a story
about coal miners, his watch stopped
working.
'Take it to George Stephenson,'
said a friend. 'He mends watches.'

So Samuel went to Stephenson's
repair shop. The walls were covered
with drawings of steam engines.
Had he come to the right place?

'Do you repair watches?' he
asked.
'Yes sir,' answered Stephenson.
'But what are all these drawings?'
asked Samuel.

'These are drawings for my steam
waggon. Only I call it a locomotive,'
said Stephenson.

'I also work in a machine shop,' Stephenson told Samuel. 'We build steam engines to pump water out of the mines. If steam engines can turn the wheels of a pump, they can turn the wheels of a waggon, too.'

Stephenson took Samuel to the machine shop. 'Look in there,' he said.

Samuel peered in. He saw men working on something. It was the locomotive!

'From my window I can see the horses pulling the coal carts along the track from the mine,' said Stephenson. 'That was what gave me the idea. A horse can pull only one cart, but an engine could pull many carts. My locomotive will do the work of many horses.'

Soon Stephenson's locomotive was ready to pull a train of coal carts from the town of Stockton to Darlington. The mine owner had built special iron rails for the train to run on.

On the day of the test, Stockton was full of people. They were all sure that the locomotive would blow up.

A man with a red face, standing near Samuel, announced
very sternly, 'Nothing will ever take the place of the horse.
These inventions are a lot of rubbish.'

'Oh please work,' prayed Samuel. 'Please, work.'
'Chuff, chuff, chuff, chuff,' sang the locomotive. It was a
beautiful sound.

'Hooray! It's working!' cried Samuel. He turned to the man with the red face, 'You, sir, are an old stick-in-the-mud!'

The train was already out of sight. Samuel jumped quickly into a horse-drawn carriage. 'Take me to Darlington!' he ordered. 'I want to greet the train when it gets there.'

He arrived neck and neck with the train. Everyone was cheering. A band was playing and people were climbing all over the train. It was a great day.

Samuel walked over to Stephenson. He was so happy that he couldn't say anything. He just hugged his friend.

The king of England was very pleased. He called all his ministers together. 'If a train can carry coal, it can carry passengers too,' he said. 'Let us build a railway from Liverpool to Manchester.'

'And let us have a contest, your Majesty,' said one of the ministers. 'Let four good judges choose the best locomotive.'

The contest took place in a railway station just outside Liverpool. Many inventors came with their locomotives.

One locomotive looked very suspicious indeed.
'Phew,' said the first judge. 'This one smells like an old horse.'
'Neigh-h-h-h-h,' said the locomotive.

'Gracious, it even sounds like an old horse,' said the second judge.

The third judge peered inside the locomotive. 'By jove, it *is* an old horse.'

The fourth judge wagged his finger at the dishonest inventor. 'You can't trick us! Leave here at once, sir.'

At the end of the day the judges chose the best locomotive. George Stephenson had won.

Work on the railway began
straight away. But it takes a long
time to build a railway, and it takes
a lot of work too. There are plans to
draw and rails to lay. There are
bridges to build and tunnels to dig.

The years were passing quickly
and Samuel Smith was getting old.
Every day he and George Stephenson
talked about the railway.

'What do you think of this design
for a bridge?' asked Stephenson.

Samuel scratched the tip of his nose, as he always did when he was thinking. 'Well,' he answered, 'let's talk about it.' They talked and talked. And late at night when everybody else was fast asleep, the two friends worked by candle-light.

On September 15th, 1830, the first passenger train was finished. Several of the king's ministers were at Liverpool to see the train leave.

The ministers all ignored Samuel. They wanted to shake George Stephenson's hand.

Stephenson looked at Samuel. 'Wish me luck old friend,' he said.

'I do, I do,' shouted Samuel as the train pulled away. His wish came true. Stephenson's train was a great success.

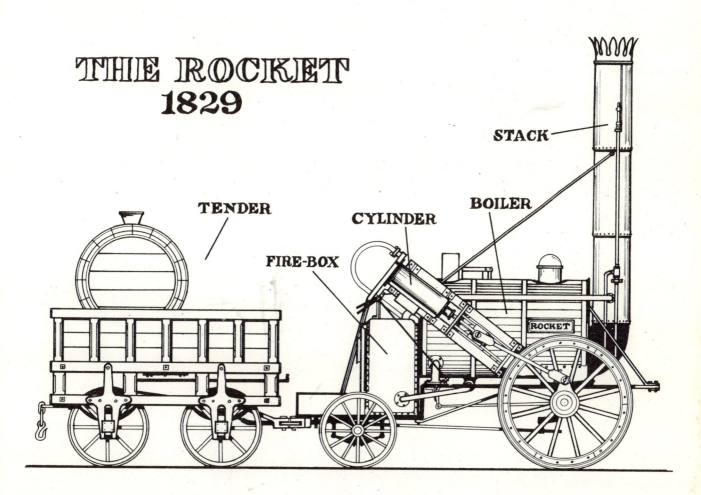